Brands & Desires

Bernd Kreutz

Hatje Cantz

How do brands come to be?

It's simple. People love music, for example. At some point, after they grew bored with whistling and singing, people began inventing ways of making music more interesting— instruments, sheet music, radio, and most recently the compact disc. Now lots of people can make all kinds of music, and lots of people all over the world can listen to it.

A global music market has emerged in the process. Makers of musical instruments compete for popularity among musicians, music labels for CD buyers, and musicians for fans. In order to ensure that producers and suppliers play fair as they battle for their respective target groups, rules have been laid down and laws passed to regulate the exchange of goods and information—from patent, copyright and trademark laws to consumer-rights legislation.

One of the most brilliant ideas was to give names to people and things. And thus Mick Jagger, Brian Jones, Keith Richards, Charlie Watts, and Bill Wyman have not spent their lives as no-name musicians but as the Rolling Stones. Thanks to all those wonderful laws, we can be sure that a CD that has the name "Rolling Stones" on it actually contains music by the Rolling Stones. And the fact that a "Mozartkugel" is a con- coction of chocolate and marzipan (enriched by the memory of a famous composer of the same name) and not a piece of music by Mozart doesn't bother us at all.

The Rolling Stones: they thrilled audiences to the point of ecstasy from the outset. Their fans were so crazy about them that they would order the next Stones album before they had even heard a single note of it. Such devotion and commitment on the part of swooning consumers is the dream of every marketing manager responsible for the launch of a new product. Desperate for that kind of success, they wonder why every name can't become a brand and what the secret is that distinguishes brands from mere names and products.

Culture analysts have long since discovered the secret behind the Rolling Stones brand. The consensus is that the Rolling Stones had a keen sense of the desires and longings of their audience: they personified its repressed aggression, urges, and ideal of coolness. The Rolling Stones were "more than a band," as their manager wrote even before their first album came out, they were a "way of life" that would give wings to the fantasies of youth.

It was desire that made the Rolling Stones objects of identification and turned them into a brand. Desire is the prerequisite for and the key to every form of brand-building. And desire is the theme of this book on brands.

RELIGION

PRODUCT & BRAND LOGO

APPLE

BRAND STORY

Steve Jobs is the Messiah. When the cofounder of Apple Computer Inc. walks onto the stage at a computer fair wearing white tennis shoes, blue jeans, and a black tee-shirt, he doesn't gaze out at a docile army of managers in dark-gray uniforms. His audience is a colorful horde of followers who leap to their feet and raise their arms in enthusiasm before he breathes his first word into the microphone.

He has been showing them the way to the Promised Land for two decades. He is the one who reveals the promises of the digital future to them. And he continually reinforces their faith: the mere sight of his products evokes an indescribable feeling of utter devotion.

Ever since the sun first rose over Silicon Valley, Steve Jobs has been the motor of technological progress. Personal computers with graphic user interfaces and a mouse, Macintosh, Powerbook, Newton, QuickTime, iMac, iPod, iTunes Music Store. He is the resurrected master who saved Apple from damnation after the infidels drove him from his CEO's chair and then led the company to the brink of ruin.

Apple is the global cult brand of the creative set. Especially in advertising, music, and film. With a market share of no more than five per cent, Apple serves a niche market, as market analysts and marketing managers are fond of saying. But in reality, Apple serves nothing and no one. Apple is a religion.

FIDELITY

DE BEERS

A DIAMOND IS FOREVER

DE BEERS

BRAND STORY

Frances Gerety had a tough problem to solve. She was preparing a presentation for De Beers of South Africa, the world's largest diamond producer. Though diamonds may be "a girl's best friend," it appeared that America hadn't gotten the message yet. Less than twenty percent of American women had a diamond ring.

That would have to change. Under the pressure to come up with a concept for success, the copywriter for the New York ad agency N. W. Ayer had put hundreds of ideas on paper already, and tossed them all out. The waste basket next to her desk was overflowing. Then she wrote down four simple words: "A diamond is forever."

But the advertising strategists had to produce more than just a slogan if they were going to win the hands of the women of America. A product placement concept, for one thing—Hollywood stars wear De Beers diamonds when they go on camera. Or the four "Cs" of diamond quality—cut, color, clarity, and carat—as criteria for grading the precious stones. Market strategy focused not least of all on spectacular, glorious high-society events like the coronation of Queen Elizabeth II as a way of heating up popular desire for the sparkling rocks.

And the strategy succeeded. By the end of the Second World War, sixty percent of all American women called a diamond ring their own—and the figure rose to seventy percent by 1980. Encouraged by their success, De Beers decided to export the tradition founded by the advertising strategists to the rest of the world as well. They began in Europe, launching an advertising campaign in 1963 that declared, more or less openly, that engagements and marriages were commitments that simply had to be celebrated with a diamond ring. De Beers sales soared once again.

Results in Japan were particularly impressive. In the late 1960s, De Beers commissioned the J. Walter Thompson agency to develop and run a campaign that would position the diamond ring as an indispensable part of the traditional Japanese wedding ceremony—with tremendous success. In 1968, only about five percent of Japanese women wore diamond rings. By 1981, the figure had risen to sixty percent.

The lifelong bond of matrimony is truly a thing of value.

MOTHER'S BREAST

MILKA

BRAND STORY

Dr. Hans Wirth was a manager who left his company more than just the obliga-tion to pay retirement benefits. When he took on the job as managing director for the chocolate producer Suchard Tobler, the firm's best-known and most important product, "Milka" whole-milk chocolate, already looked back on seven-ty years of marketing success. That was a genuine challenge for Dr. Wirth.

He engaged the services of Young & Rubicam, an advertising agency with offices in Frankfurt. There he encountered in Uwe Ortstein, Sandor Szabo, and Ilse Theisen a creative team that was perfectly suited to his tastes. In the spirit of "make the new familiar and the familiar new," the trio developed an ad campaign featuring photographs tinted in the same shade of purple used on the paper wrapping of the chocolate. At some point, the three hit upon the idea of "paint-ing" the cow purple as well, with white lettering on its hide. The cow appears with an alpine farmer against a background of snow-topped peaks on every Milka package.

The name "Milka" is derived from "MILk" and "KAkao" (German for "cocoa"). Company founder Philippe Suchard is known as one of the inventors of milk chocolate.

Dr. Wirth saw the potential of the purple cow and encouraged the creative team to eliminate all embellishment and focus entirely on the motif of the purple cow—in ads, billboards, TV commercials, and promotions.

The company was later bought out by Jacobs and subsequently by Philip Morris. The purple cow remained the single constant and has become the trademark for a whole family of products that now includes several dozen items.

The serenity of the Swiss mountain countryside, the symbols of untainted nature, the image of an amusing purple cow with a golden cowbell around its neck and a full udder with two teats identify Milka as "the most tender temptation since chocolate was invented."

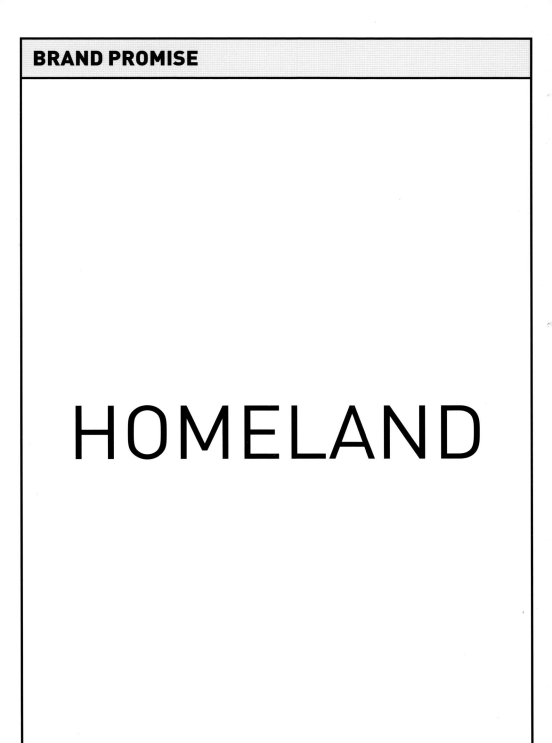

HOMELAND

ROTHAUS

BRAND STORY

Dr. Norbert Nothhelfer opens his mail folder as he does every morning. As on almost every other day, there is nothing but good news. The best is always on the top of the stack. Today, he finds an article from the highly respected German news magazine *Der Spiegel*. The first two paragraphs read as follows:

"Norbert Nothhelfer recently received another letter from a faraway place. This one came from Afghanistan. Along with a few friendly lines addressed to the director of the Rothaus Brewing Company, the letter contained a photograph, a picture of a group of German Army soldiers taken in the Hindukush region. The troops are shown smiling brightly and raising small bottles of pilsner beer into the air. Clearly visible on the labels is a Black Forest maiden in traditional costume, apple-cheeked and smiling happily. A rather down-home image, actually. The soldiers are paying tribute to "Tannenzäpfle" (pine cone), the local beer brewed in their homeland in the mountains of the Black Forest. Nothhelfer received the same kind of mail from Kosovo. Troops stationed there were equally reluctant to go without their traditional brew from South Baden. Since taking over the company eleven years before, annual revenue had risen from 27 million Euros to nearly 70 million. And twenty-eight percent of that is net profit."

The Rothaus Brewery was founded by the Benedictine monastery in St. Blasien in 1792. In the wake of secularization and abolition of the monarchy, it eventually became a state-owned enterprise run by the German state of Baden-Württemberg and has since been registered as the "Badische Staatsbrauerei Rothaus AG." The brewery is located in Rothaus, a town in the southern Black Forest, one of the most beautiful vacation spots in Germany. It is a quiet, peaceful, healthy setting in the heart of nature.

The brewery's success is the product of a business concept that is not just conservative but arch-conservative. In Baden-Württemberg, being arch-conservative means sticking to what you know how to do but doing it better and consistently better than everyone else. In beer production, that means superior raw materials, superior product quality, state-of-the-art production and bottling facilities, exemplary environmental awareness, and satisfied, highly motivated employees. In terms of product policy, it means no experiments. The company has produced exactly six types of beer from the very beginning. Beer is filled in bottles only, never in small cans or large kegs. And there are no trendy beer-and-soft-drink mixes. In product and marketing policy, arch-conservatism means fair prices and fair partnerships. In financial policy, it means avoiding debts, because debts make a company dependent on others. In brand policy, it means trusting in the strength of the brand and knowing that a reputation for quality gets around. If you are patient and a bit lucky, customers will become loyal customers, and loyal customers will become fans who form communities and celebrate with Rothaus beer—served by "Beergit," the smiling Black Forest girl dressed in traditional local garb shown on the brand label in front of two green fir trees beneath the historical Baden coat of arms, holding two brightly shining beer glasses invitingly at her breast. That is homeland.

BRAND STORY

Susan Parker, eighteen, from Calgary, is about to start college and needs book-shelves, a desk, and a bed—all as inexpensive as possible, of course.

Hans Schmidt, twenty-one, from Nuremberg, can hardly wait to move in with his girlfriend. It will be their first shared apartment. All they lack is a sofabed, some kitchen cupboards, and a set of living room chairs—but no long wait for delivery, please!

Lin Tse-Hsiu, twenty-seven, from Shanghai, has just become a father and needs a cradle, a playpen, and a chest of drawers. He doesn't have to run from one furniture store to the next—because now there's an Ikea in Shanghai.

Lenka Sukova, seventy-six, from Prague, wants to surprise her grandson with a new CD rack for his birthday, and she knows just where to get it—at Ikea, where else?

Ingvar Kamprad, seventeen, from Agunnaryd, had an idea about how to make people happy—people with a variety of different needs, requirements, tastes, and budgets. The idea that prompted the Ikea founder to start furnishing the world, from his home town of Agunnaryd to Adelaide, was as simple as it was astounding. He set up a self-service furniture store and began designing furniture people could buy in modules and then pick up, assemble and install themselves. It was also a concept that enabled Ikea to sell at prices no competitor could match.

Success was not long in coming. The small operation in a little Swedish town grew up and became a global giant. While the traditional furniture business was battling with dwindling sales, Ikea went on opening one new branch after another, doubling annual revenue roughly every five years. The key figures for 2002 tell the story: 177 furniture stores in thirty-one countries, 118 million Ikea catalogs in print, 287 million Ikea shoppers, and eleven billion euros in turnover.

Although Ikea has achieved the transformation from an outsider to a trend brand, it still embodies a sense of new beginnings and belief in the future—and maybe a few sparks of the entrepreneurial spirit that prompted young Ingvar to embark on the Ikea adventure.

IKEA

GROWING UP

BRAND STORY

Daniel and Markus Freitag leaned against the kitchen window in their communal apartment in West Zurich, gazing out at the Hardbrücke and watching the endless stream of trucks rumbling across the bridge on their way from Germany to Italy and back.

Daniel and Markus were thinking about life. Both had just completed their vocational training and now had a burning desire to get out and do their own thing. Their parents were devoted environmentalists, and the sons had developed a critical attitude toward consumption and the throwaway society. They had been toying for some time with the idea of producing something, recycling something, and breathing new life into old stuff. The only problem was: what?

But right then, Daniel and Markus had another problem, a much more urgent one. They needed practical bags they could sling over their shoulders as they rode their bicycles to work every day. And they couldn't find any that suited them.

His eye on the Hardbrücke, Markus said to Daniel, "Why don't we try something with truck tarpaulins." A female friend of theirs was a seamstress and had an old industrial sewing machine she was willing to lend them. Daniel and Markus salvaged a piece of used truck tarp from a local hauling firm, got an old bicycle inner tube, and picked up a length of car seat belt from a junkyard. From these materials, they sewed their first shoulder bag.

Not only do the Freitags make the bags themselves, they also do everything else. Trademark, packaging design, trade fair stands, shop design, public relations— all are Freitag productions. Their Web shop at *www.freitag.ch* is a labor of love. The only thing they leave to others—a law firm with eighty names on its letterhead—are the legal disputes with product pirates all over the world. As their own target group, they have no need for market research. And classical advertising would be a waste of money, perhaps even counterproductive.

Today, the Freitag brothers are represented by licensed dealerships all over Europe, in Japan, the U.S., Australia, and Asia. Every product is a one-of-a-kind article. Freitag is the ultimate brand for extreme individualists and environmentally aware followers of fashion.

FREITAG

INDI-VIDUALISM

FREEDOM

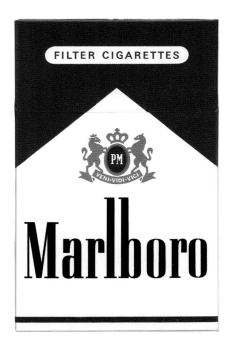

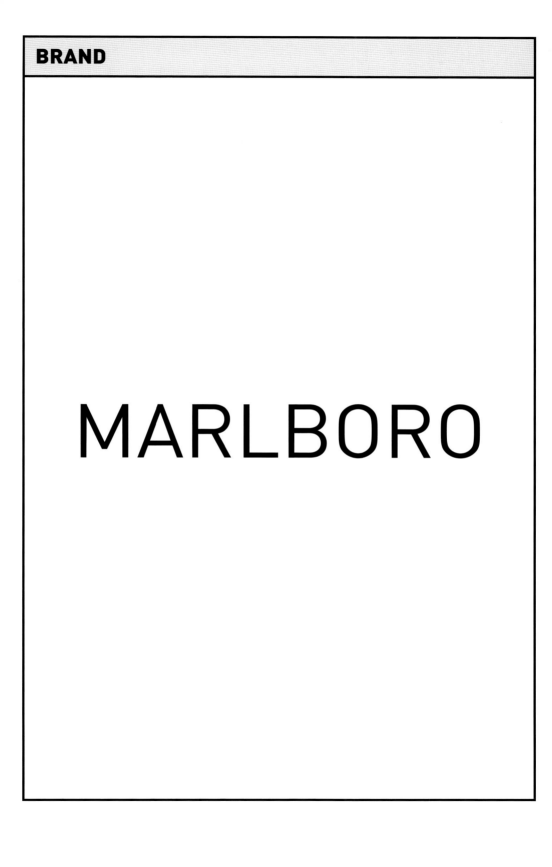

MARLBORO

BRAND STORY

Leo Burnett had just turned sixty-three. Sitting in the conference room of his Chicago ad agency were several executives of Philip Morris Inc. of New York, and they had brought him a tough problem to solve.

Marlboro, one of their cigarette brands, had been a so-so seller for some thirty years. The brand was positioned in the high-price segment and smoked primarily by women.

Philip Morris had decided to launch a campaign using the Marlboro name to gain a larger share of the mid-price mass market segment that catered mainly to male consumers.

Leo Burnett's job was to harness the resources of mass communication to establish Marlboro as a men's cigarette that women like as well. The PM executives had laid the groundwork, ordering up a stronger tobacco mixture, adding a filter to what had been a non-filter cigarette, and developing a packaging innovation—the flip-top box—that took Burnett by surprise.

Burnett's first ad shows America's number-one symbol of robust manhood, the portrait of a cowboy with a cigarette in his mouth. The caption reads: "New from Philip Morris. Marlboro filter cigarettes." On the lower left is an open flip-top box, and a brief, factual text lists the benefits of the new product in straightforward language.

The product relaunch was a complete success. Riding the success of Hollywood westerns, Marlboro became an export hit. People everywhere—all "dependent" in one way or another—reached for the pack with the red triangle and the name that expresses the vision of freedom: "Come to where the flavor is. Come to Marlboro Country."

Philip Morris was extremely grateful to Leo Burnett. Never before in the history of business had so many billions of dollars been earned with a single brand idea.

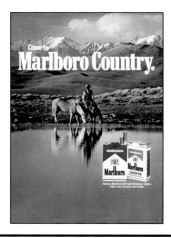

JUSTICE

BENETTON

BRAND STORY

Rosa Benetton once said in an interview, "My children tell me that these photos appeal to young people and most of all that they prompt people to talk about the brand. That is advertising for us, but I'm not comfortable with it. My children should stop doing that, or I'll get very angry. They simply have to stop doing that."

By that time, her children, Luciano, Giuliana, Gilberto, and Carlo, had built out of nothing a textile firm with 6,000 shops in 100 countries pulling in 1.6 billion dollars of turnover a year—and Mama was angry. Yet she could well have been proud of her kids. Their idea of producing woolen knitwear in huge lots and dyeing them at the very last minute in the newest colors of the season had revolutionized the textile industry. And their exclusive franchise shops had revolutionized the retail clothing businesses as well. Did Mama really think that Luciano, her eldest, was going to stick to conventional approaches forever—especially when it came to advertising, his own specialty? For a few years he actually had. But in 1984, frustrated by the lackluster products of his ad agencies, he went to photographer Oliviero Toscani for help.

Toscani had a very simple lead idea: "All the Colors of the World." The first ads showed smiling children and adolescents of all skin colors and ethnic groups happily united in brightly colored, fashionable Benetton outfits. Luciano found them terrific, and so did retailers, customers, the media, and the public. But Luciano wouldn't have been Luciano and Toscani wouldn't have been Toscani if they had left it at that.

Step by step, they shaped the most eye-catching, widely discussed, controversial ad campaign in advertising history. The ads no longer focused on fashion but on such themes as love and suffering, sex and religion, war and persecution, crime and the environment, birth and death. United Colors of Benetton became the most popular fashion brand in the world, its founders some of the richest people in Italy.

On April 29, 2000, Luciano split with Toscani after sixteen years of fertile symbiosis. It was his mother's eighty-seventh birthday. Rosa Benetton, née Carniato, died three days later.

RESPECT

MERCEDES-BENZ

BRAND STORY

Janis Joplin sang, "Oh lord, won't you buy me a Mercedes Benz / My friends all drive Porsches, I must make amends / Worked hard all my lifetime, no help from my friends / So oh lord, won't you buy me a Mercedes Benz."

Janis Joplin didn't want a Cadillac, a Rolls-Royce, or a Ferrari. No, she begged God to give her a "Mercedes Benz."

The object of her starry-eyed longing first appeared on an ad poster for Mercedes-Benz in 1929. Of course, it didn't show a woman who had worked hard all her life and still couldn't afford a Mercedes. Instead, the illustration condenses all of the ideas people have of leisure and luxury into an image of a pleasant summer night on the Côte d'Azur. A beautiful blonde in a strapless red evening gown lounges in a wicker chair, gazing transfixed at a Mercedes star shining brightly in the middle of the nighttime sky.

The aura associated with the Mercedes-Benz brand remains as strong as ever today. In retrospect, Jürgen E. Schrempp, the brain behind the merger of Daimler-Benz and Chrysler and its present CEO, describes its rational underpinnings in the following words:

"The names Gottlieb Daimler and Karl Benz, the founders of Daimler-Benz, are closely associated with the invention of the automobile. The history of the automobile began with Daimler's first motor coach and the Benz three-wheeler in 1886. Daimler positioned his cars early on at the high end of the scale in terms of quality, dependability, safety, and comfort. Cars bearing the name "Mercedes," which was registered at the patent office in 1902, and the three-pointed star were driven in the early years by prominent figures in social, cultural, and business life. Milestones in the company's one-hundred-and-ten-year history include numerous pioneering inventions—the first bus produced by Karl Benz (1895), the first truck developed by Gottlieb Daimler (1896), the first taxicab (1896/97), the shiftable gear transmission developed in 1889, and the honeycomb radiator first produced in 1900, to name only a few. The earliest Mercedes, designed around the turn of the century, is generally regarded today as the first modern automobile. Daimler-Benz has been a pioneer and pacesetter for all other advances in race-car design as well as passenger safety ever since."

As important as these accomplishments may be, they do not suffice to explain the unparalleled success of Mercedes-Benz. The brand has succeeded, on a global scale and across all class boundaries, in transforming its objective achievements into social recognition for its customers.

MANLINESS

VICTORINOX

BRAND STORY

Karl Elsener had eleven brothers and sisters. As the fourth eldest, with no prospect of taking over his parents' millinery firm and hat shop in Ibach in the canton of Schwyz, he learned the cutler's trade and opened his own workshop on January 1, 1884. Karl Elsener was not only a craftsman but also a born entrepreneur. Unwilling to accept the Swiss Army's policy of having its pocket knives produced in Germany, he founded the Swiss Master Cutlers' Association and parlayed the organization's strength to bring the contract for the military knives back to Switzerland.

But Karl Elsener had other talents. A gifted inventor as well, he developed a number of novel ideas for the design of the soldier's knife and patented a six-part "officer's knife" in 1897. Though it was not part of standard Swiss Army issue, the knife quickly became extremely popular and thus naturally attracted imitators. To set his product apart from these imitations, Elsener decided to emboss a Swiss coat of arms on the product. After the death of his mother, he made her name—Victoria—the company trademark. With the advent of stainless steel, known as Inox, in 1921, his sons converted to the new material and created the company and brand name that has lasted until today: *Victorinox*.

After World War II, U.S. Army, Navy, and Air Force post exchanges sold "Swiss Army Knives" by the thousands to enlisted personnel and officers. U.S. Presidents Johnson, Reagan, and Bush had the "Classic" model imprinted with a gold-plated presidential seal and presented the knives as gifts to White House visitors. NASA put the knife in the kits its astronauts took along on their space flights. Over the years, the original "officer's knife" spawned a diverse range of products fitted with a variety additional tools.

The Victorinox brand combines all of the positive associations people have with Switzerland: originality and quality, precision and reliability, safety and discipline, orderliness and cleanliness. But the Victorinox name is also linked with the mythos of the Swiss Army, with all of its unique aspects: universal military service with annual training, soldiers who keep their equipment, weapons, and ammunition at home, and a special spirit of camaraderie that crosses over into civilian life. The Swiss Army Knife symbolizes the inventiveness and resolve of the individual left to fend for himself.

FAIRNESS

PRODUCT & BRAND LOGO

eBay

BRAND STORY

Pierre Omidyar is not a businessman, he is a programmer. And he is a person with ideals. People with ideals do not get excited about business plans, they get excited about ideas. One day, Pierre Omidyar had an idea of his own, and he found it exciting: online auctions. And because he knew how to program, there was nothing to stop him from putting his idea to work. AuctionWeb went online under the domain *www.ebay.com*.

Omidyar realized that the Internet provided the perfect way of linking people who want to sell something with people who are looking for something. His AuctionWeb is a virtual marketplace that brings demand and supply together in a fair and democratic way. In order to ensure that the system works, he offers a piece of advice at his Website that reminds us of Immanuel Kant's Categorical Imperative: "Deal with others the way you would have them deal with you. Remember that you are usually dealing with individuals, just like yourself. Subject to making mistakes. Well-meaning, but wrong on occasion. That's just human."

Since Omidyar is not a businessman, he does not speak of *customers* but of *community*. He gives the community the sense that the man behind the scenes is not a slick profiteer but someone who understands their interests and needs and takes them seriously. He communicates with them like a good neighbor and gives them a forum in which to communicate with each other. And thus the community is perfectly willing to pay a fair price for the new service. The community has grown from seventy people to seventy million. And because Omidyar has known right along that he is not a businessman, he wasted no time putting the management of eBay in the hands of a very good businesswoman, Meg Whitman.

And by the way, if you, the reader, have never experienced eBay, you ought to do yourself the favor. Sell this book, and remember that your chances of selling it are better, the more you praise it. But your praise has to be honest. And you can do the author a favor as well by letting him know how much you get for it—by e-mail to: berndkreutz@hotmail.com

VITALITY

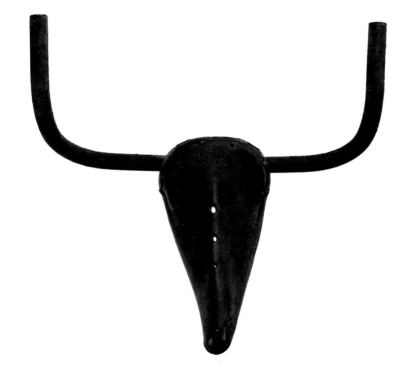

PICASSO

BRAND STORY

Pablo Picasso inherited a talent from his father: he could paint. But lots of others could paint, too, and if he was going to become a professional artist and succeed at it, he would have to decide on a direction. The market had three models to offer: past, present, and future.

He studied the representatives of the past and benefited from their example as he trained, practicing until he achieved perfect command of the craft. But the past, as he soon realized, was not his thing. So he proceeded to imitate representatives of the present—Pissarro, Toulouse-Lautrec, Munch, Degas, Cézanne. But he literally saw no future in that, either. One doesn't become a brand with me-too products. Thus he decided, for lack of a better choice, to go with the model of the future.

As a gifted marketing man, he knew that his first job would be to develop a unique product. And so he invented Cubism. He put the marketing of his new product category in the hands of a Paris art dealer named Daniel-Henry Kahnweiler. The two worked out a pricing strategy that put Picasso at the high end of the market. Although that limited sales potential early on, the strategy would lead to a sales explosion once the new style of art gained a foothold. Kahnweiler took an extremely selective approach to sales. He sold only to collectors and museums he knew would be good for Picasso's reputation and his future market value.

The communication concept used to establish Picasso in the market relied on a network of friends, patrons, buyers, fellow artists and intellectuals, on selective participation in group exhibitions of avant-garde artists, and on solo shows in prominent galleries and museums. Following initial success in France, the duo of Picasso/Kahnweiler applied the concept to all of the other important markets abroad. The plan worked. By the age of twenty-five, Picasso was a made man. But he kept moving. Driven by boundless energy, he invented one new form of expression after the other, not only in paintings, but in drawings, and collages, sculptures and ceramics as well. He made his many marriages and love affairs as much a focus of public attention as his embrace of communism. His artistic potency and dominance, coupled with his ability to position himself with optimum effect in the media eye, took him through the stages of the brand-building process in rapid order: recognition, respect, familiarity, fame, and mythos.

Picasso rose from beginnings as an impoverished painter to the status of a brand worth billions. Decades after his death, the automobile manufacturer Citroën purchased the right to decorate its Xsara model with the Picasso brand name—at a price so high that the parties to the contract agreed to keep it secret.

ACTION

RED BULL

BRAND STORY

Chaleo Yoovidhya was a highly respected businessman in Thailand. Among other things, his family-owned company T.C. Pharmaceutical Industries produced "Krating Daeng," a popular energy drink sold as a pick-me-up in small brown bottles in Thailand. *Krating Daeng* is Thai for "red bull." It took a simple signature on a piece of paper to make Yoovidhya one of the four hundred richest people in the world (according to *Forbes Magazine*).

The Austrian Dietrich Mateschitz was a marketing manager earning a good salary at a German subsidiary of Procter & Gamble. He was introduced to "Krating Daeng" as a remedy for jet lag on a business trip to Asia. He immediately got in touch with Chaleo Yoovidhya. Mateschitz had a vision and a personal mission. He saw a market for energy drinks like "Krating Daeng" in the non-Asian world, and he also wanted to start his own business. Yoovidhya became his partner by signing his name.

Dietrich Mateschitz turned out to be a marketing genius and a born entrepreneur. The name of the product was quickly chosen: "Red Bull." Nor did the packaging—a slim aluminum can—or the packaging design take long to develop.

The matter of adapting the original recipe to European taste buds was a bit more difficult. And the differences in national requirements for approvals of foods and beverages for sale posed a real problem. But Mateschitz overcame every obstacle with enthusiasm, passion, and commitment.

Red Bull was introduced to the Austrian market in 1987. It was positioned as a lifestyle beverage, priced eight times higher than Coca-Cola, and supported by an unconventional ad campaign designed by his long-time friend Johannes Kastner, a highly respected advertising specialist in Germany. His slogan "Red Bull gives you wings" quickly became a watchword. Aggressive product sampling and imaginative event marketing made Red Bull the favorite drink of an "in crowd" obsessed with enjoying life, a target group that combined dynamism and productivity in school and professional life with dedication to the ultimate kick in leisure activities.

The firm's involvement in Formula 1 racing, sponsoring commitments to extreme and fun sports and their scene stars, as well as unconventional events of its own, such as the Red Bull Flight Festivals, have since helped shape Red Bull's image in seventy countries as an energy drink that invigorates the mind and the body and as a brand that unites success with action and fun.

EASY GOING

CAMPER

BRAND STORY

Lorenzo Fluxá was determined to go his own way. Instead of taking over the shoe factory his great-grandfather Antonio had founded in Inca on the Balearic Island of Mallorca in 1877, he started his own business in 1975. And from the outset, he set himself apart from his competitors in practically every way.

Starting with his choice of a name for the company: *Camper* means "farmer" in Mallorquín—not a particularly trendy concept. Nor was the product. His first collection was inspired by the traditional shoes worn by the local rural population. His materials—canvas, suede, and rubber—were not especially hip. And his communication strategy was anything but fashion conscious. The general theme "Camper. The Walking Society" and the slogan "Walk—don't run" have the tone of an anti-modernist manifesto that rejects the dynamism, acceleration, and continuous change that characterize modern society. Starting with a simple pair of shoes, Lorenzo Fluxá created a "way of walking" over the years. He exported this Mediterranean mentality to the urban jungles of the world's big cities. Health consciousness and environmental awareness, social responsibility, and respect for tradition are combined in *Camper* with a mixture of primal *joie de vivre,* unlimited imagination, and interest in the new. Earnestness is paired with humor, wit with irony, business success with cultural commitment.

Going through life on one's own two feet, one's head held high, and being true to one's self without getting into a sweat—that is the philosophy that virtually no other brand embodies as effectively as *Camper.*

IMAGINATION

ABSOLUT

BRAND STORY

Lars Lindmark, the new president of V&S Vin & Sprit AB in the Swedish city of Åhus imagined this: If the potential for growth in our strictly regulated home market is limited, then we should try to sell a premium vodka in the country where sixty percent of the vodka produced in the world is consumed. America here we come.

Gunnar Broman and colleagues, Lindmark's Swedish advertising experts, imagined this: If all the vodka bottles in the world look like Russian church spires and have symbols of czarist heraldry on their labels, then we should fill our vodka in simple cylindrical bottles like the ones pharmacists have been using to hold alcohol for centuries. We should also eliminate the label altogether and print right on the bottle. And we should call the product *Absolut Vodka*.

Geoff Hayes, Art Director at the New York ad agency TBWA imagined this: an ad with a full-frame photograph of a crystal-clear bottle of Absolut crowned with a halo. His copywriter Graham Turner imagined "Absolut perfection." as the absolute headline. Bill Tragos, the "T" in TBWA, imagined this: This idea gives us the potential of "Absolut something." Michel Roux of Carillon Importers imagined this: If I can get Andy to paint the bottle, it would be "Absolut Warhol." and an absolute sensation. And thus, the themes of the Absolut product, Absolut objects, Absolut cities, Absolut fashion—to mention only a few—generated hundreds of motifs and one of the most creative and effective series of ads in the history of advertising. And collaboration with dozens of artists from all over the world gave rise to a unique cultural dialog.

The "bottom line"—and this almost defies imagination—is that volume sales of Absolut Vodka rose from 90,000 liters in 1979 to 67 million liters (worldwide) in 2002.

Clarity, simplicity, perfection—a successful concept for Absolut but also a sure-fire recipe for the successful brand per se.

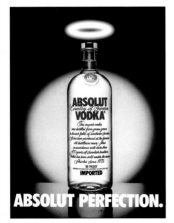

FANTASY

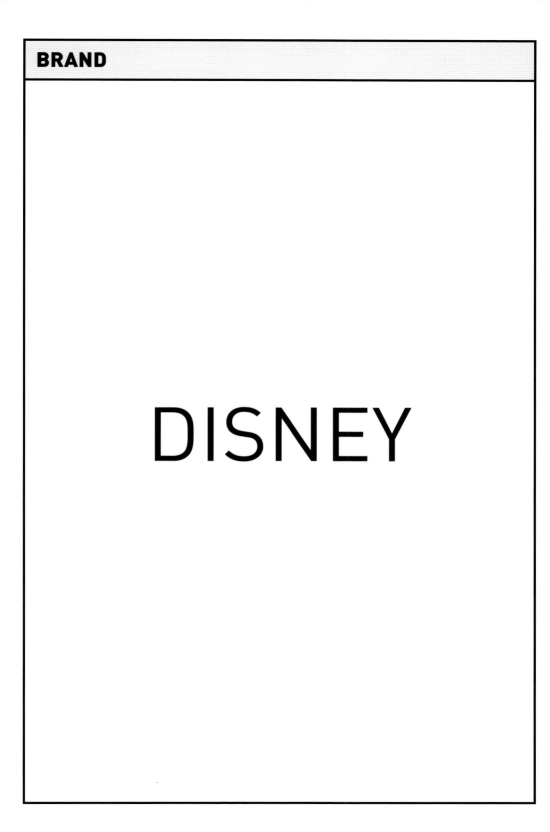

DISNEY

BRAND STORY

Michael D. Eisner, Chairman and CEO of The Walt Disney Company, wrote the following words in a letter to the shareholders in the company's 2002 annual report: "There are two principal attributes that make a brand powerful from a business perspective. It must be unique—and it must be relevant. Uniqueness is the quality that determines the ability to use the brand to differentiate one's products. In this sense, the Disney brand is truly unique. However, to be commercially powerful, a brand must also be relevant to consumers. Clearly, Disney passes this test. Disney is about family, fun and fantasy."

Michael D. Eisner is the head of a media and entertainment group that employed 112,000 people and generated turnover of 25 billion dollars in 2002—figures that prompt us to recall a remark once made by its founding father Walter Elias Disney: "I only hope that we don't lose sight of one thing—that it was all started by a mouse." Mickey Mouse debuted in *Steamboat Willy,* the first fully synchronized animated cartoon. Mickey Mouse was Walt Disney's creation. He was born on Disney's sketchbook, and Disney lent him his voice. People close to Walt even say that he put his soul into Mickey as well.

Disney was not only a gifted cartoonist, director, and producer, he was also an attentive and farsighted businessman. He immediately reinvested proceeds from distribution and merchandising in new projects, new employees, new studios, and the development of new technologies. Thirteen of his thirty-two Academy Awards were given to him personally for technical innovations.

The opening of Disneyland in Anaheim, California, and his determined commitment to the new medium of television, illustrate on a grand scale Disney's talent for creating profit from fantasy and using that profit with imagination. Michael D. Eisner clearly has that same talent. He gave the company a new structure, expanded into new fields of business, and raised the price of Disney stock to new, fantastic heights.

Even if shares are just pieces of printed paper, as Scrooge McDuck would say, they are eloquent evidence of the potential a brand can develop if it is guided by someone who understands it.

HARMONY

WELEDA

BRAND STORY

Rudolf Steiner was a philosopher, educator, and scientist. He has gone down in history as the founder of anthroposophy (which means something like "human wisdom") and the Anthroposophical Society and as the director of the Free University for the Humanities. Steiner designed the school's main complex, the Goetheanum in Dornach, Switzerland, himself. It is a prototype of organic building that has influenced many prominent architects. Anthroposophic thought and insights have had a fertilizing effect on many areas of life: in agriculture (organic food production), in education (as represented by Waldorf Schools and their emphasis on individual freedom), in the theory of movement (eurythmics), and in medicine and pharmacy.

Steiner's early lectures on the anthroposophic approach to medicine offered many stimulating ideas about medications, dietetics, and cosmetics and generated strong demand for such products. Consequently, new laboratories and companies devoted to research, development, and production of products outside the sphere of academic pharmacy began to spring up everywhere.

Weleda AG was formed through a merger of several of these enterprises in 1922. "Weleda" was an ancient Germanic seer and healer. The idea of reviving her as a corporate name originated with Rudolf Steiner.

According to Steiner, the human being, as an advanced natural species, finds substances and processes in nonhuman nature, i.e. in plants, minerals, and animals, that are related to the human organism, its organ system, and its organs. The powers contained in these substances can, alone or in combination, help to preserve or restore mental, emotional, and physical harmony in the human being.

On the basis of this principle, Weleda produces a wide range of health supplements and care products which contain no synthetic preservatives, dyes, or aromatic substances and are not tested on animals, as is standard practice in the pharmaceutical industry. These products include natural medications for a variety of different disorders, dietetic preparations, and a broad spectrum of facial and body care products.

An increasing number of people all over the world, including many who neither subscribe to anthroposophy nor are interested in karma and reincarnation, seek a life of harmony with nature and find in Weleda a brand that conforms with their views on life.

PERFECTION

STRADIVARI

BRAND STORY

Antonio Stradivari left the world 540 violins, 50 cellos, 12 violas, and an unsolved mystery. The mystery was the secret of what makes a Stradivari a Stradivari, while all other violins, cellos, and violas are just violins, cellos, and violas.

The materials, designs, and techniques Stradivari used were available to all other violin-makers of his time. The same goes for the know-how. And like his direct rival Andrea Guarneri and many of his other colleagues in the trade, he learned his craft under the tutelage of Nicola Amati in Cremona.

Contemporaries with a rather more technical orientation tend to attribute Stradivari's secret to a simple formula: the secret composition of the golden-yellow varnish he used for the finishing coat on his instruments. People with a background in art history have a different explanation: the golden section as the basis for a new violin shape based upon a harmony of proportions. Musicians, on the other hand, see the solution of the puzzle as a matter of acoustics. They swear to the unmistakable, inimitable "Cremona sound." And even Simone Sacconi, who really ought to know best—he is the leading violin-maker of our time, has repaired over 350 Stradivaris with his own hands, and has produced instruments that have been mistaken by other experts for original Stradivaris—has no other explanation for Stradivari's secret than the perfection of every part of the instrument: the fingerboard, the tailpiece, the bass-bar, the scroll, et cetera.

Antonio Stradivari has lain in his grave for more than 250 years. Yet Antonio Stradivari is still very much alive in our midst—in his products and their sound, in the Stradivari mythos and the Stradivari brand.

SURPRISE

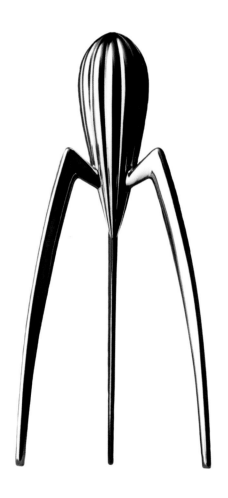

S+ARCK®

STARCK

BRAND STORY

Philippe Starck designs toothbrushes and flyswatters, sofas and bathtubs, lamps and doorknobs, shoes and handbags, motorcycles and boats. He furnishes bars and restaurants, aircraft and hotels. He builds office buildings and factories. His works are made of plastic and aluminum, steel and concrete, wood and marble. But more importantly, they are filled with feeling and imagination. And with these qualities he generates either attention, interest, the urge to buy, pleasure, and devotion—or bafflement, rejection, and hate.

Some call Philippe Starck a designer, interior architect, and architect. Others say, no, he is a decorator, a provocateur, a con man. Still others see him as an inventor, an engineer, and an entrepreneur. Not true, says the next group: He is an artist, a philosopher, a child. And then there are those who call him a genius, a poet, and a magician. They are all wrong.

Starck is a brand, a brand that promises surprise—for clients, purchasers, the media, and the public alike. The brand has never disappointed them, has never promised more than it could deliver, and has never failed to be worth the money paid for it. The Starck brand is now so powerful that people regard it as capable of anything and will believe whatever it promises— provided it is a surprise and the Starck brand logo appears large enough on that surprise.

The brand has emancipated itself from its creator. Now Philippe Starck, the man, can finally get some sleep.

RESISTANCE

PRODUCT & BRAND LOGO

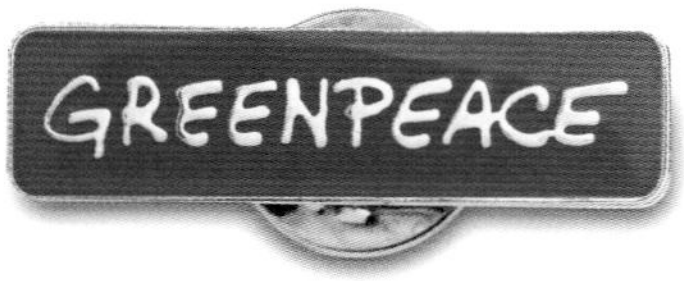

GREENPEACE

BRAND STORY

Fernando Pereira died for a good cause. The photographer drowned on July 10, 1985 in Auckland harbor when the French secret service bombed and sank the "Rainbow Warrior." The ship was just about to embark on a journey to protest the French nuclear weapon testing on the Moruroa Atoll. Fernando Pereira died on assignment for Greenpeace.

Humanity faces many dangers and threats: nuclear weapons tests, acid rain, the ozone hole, toxic waste transports, the wholesale slaughtering of seals, tanker disasters, purse seine fishing, diluted-acid dumping on the high seas, whaling, nuclear power plant accidents, rain forest destruction, genetic engineering, pesticides, dioxin, fluorocarbons, and so on and so forth. But there is only one organization dedicated to battling them all.

Greenpeace was founded in Vancouver in 1972 by three anti-nuclear power activists, Jim Bohlen, Irving Stowe, and Paul Cote. Since then, the organization has committed itself to preserving the basic foundations of life on our planet—forcefully but nonviolently. Hardly a month goes by without news of a spectacular action somewhere in the world: Greenpeace activists blocking an oil tanker with inflatable rubber boats, chaining themselves to rails ahead of trains carrying nuclear waste, occupying drilling rigs, or boycotting filling station chains. Virtually no other organization is capable of identifying its opponents so precisely, isolating them so completely, and forcing them to show their colors in the confrontation.

The small founding group has since grown. Greenpeace now has forty-three well-structured, globally networked national associations and three million members. It is the largest environmentalist organization in the world. It is a counterweight to official policy, a feared opponent of big business, a specter of horror for trade associations, and an advocate for consumers and nature. Greenpeace is a brand and a banner under which three million heroes rally, united in their belief in a cause they are willing to fight for and dedicate their lives to.

REBELLION

BRAND STORY

Richard Branson had just turned twenty-one when he opened a record shop on London's Oxford Street: *Virgin Records.* He was not intimidated by the overpowering competition.

Richard Branson was only twenty-two when the first album by the first artist signed by his newly founded record label *Virgin Music* became a worldwide hit: Mike Oldfield's *Tubular Bells*, an album that made music history. Virtually overnight, the established big players in the music industry had a new competitor, one they hadn't counted on and one they would have to take seriously.

Richard Branson was just thirty-three when he founded *Virgin Atlantic Airways*, driving national monopolist British Airways to the brink of desperation.

Richard Branson was just forty-four when he introduced *Virgin Cola* to the British market to the dismay of global market leaders Coca-Cola and Pepsi.

Richard Branson had just turned forty-eight when he published the first part of his autobiography. In the book he writes: "I am often asked where the limits for Virgin are and whether we haven't put too much of a burden on the name. I am constantly being reminded that no other company in the world would lend its name to such a mixed bag of products and companies. The people who offer these arguments are right, and I am proud of it."

The idea for the brand name "Virgin" came from one of Branson's employees. "How about Virgin? We certainly are virgins in this business," she said. "Fantastic," replied Richard Branson, "Virgin is a great name." The trademark was designed by Trevor Key. He had been doodling on a napkin during a meeting. Branson happened to look over his shoulder and said, "That's it." So Trevor presented his bill: 200 pounds.

MOVING UP

BECKHAM

BRAND STORY

David Beckham called a press conference to announce his transfer from Manchester United to Real Madrid. 547 journalists and thirty-nine TV camera teams were on hand. The event was broadcast in sixty-three countries and followed live by more than two billion viewers. These figures alone make it clear that what happened here was not a soccer player changing clubs but a brand moving to a new distribution channel. "He comes from the Theater of Dreams, Old Trafford Stadium, to the Dream Team," remarked Madrid's president Florentino Perez in his welcoming address.

David Beckham's roots are lower middle class. As the son of a kitchen fitter and a hairstylist, he grew up in London's Leytonstone district. He began his career as a soccer player in Manchester United's youth program. He signed his first professional contract at age eighteen and celebrated eight English Premiership, a Champions League, and a World Cup victory in the following years.

But it takes more than a top performance record to make a world-class brand. That is only the first prerequisite. The added value in Beckham's case is a fascinating mix of youth, good looks, money, success, health, extravagance, and personal happiness. His marriage to "Posh Spice" Victoria Adams, a member of the most successful girl group in the world, made Beckham the first pop star in the history of soccer. The combination creates an aura that virtually no one can ignore.

David Beckham does it all. He is a soccer star and a media star, an animal in bed (to quote Mrs. Beckham), and a loving father. David Beckham has it all: luxury cars and mansions, governesses and butlers. David Beckham plays every role: the shy boy from next door and the fashion model in a lightning storm of camera flashes, the dream man for many women, and the dream woman for more than a few men.

David Beckham has so many things that so many other people don't have. He is what a lot of millionaires would give their eye teeth to be. That is why they adore him. And that is why so many companies offer him so much money. They want to bathe in a little of the fame, the splendor, and the glory he radiates—even if they ultimately remain the same second-rate wanna-bes they always were.

THE ELITE

HARVARD BUSINESS SCHOOL

BRAND STORY

George W. Bush is President of the United States of America. He is also a graduate of Harvard Business School—like many of the women and men in top positions in business, education, and politics today. No other school in the world is as well known and as highly respected as Harvard Business School.

Founded in 1908, the school has awarded more than 40,000 degrees to graduates who have been privileged to harvest the latest fruits of management research and management theory available at a given time. It is one of the first business schools to offer both an MBA degree and an "Executive Education" program for working managers. The case-study method developed at Harvard during the 1920s still offers the most practical approach to business education.

Of course these facts alone do not fully explain what makes Harvard Business School so extraordinarily attractive to companies, students, and the general public. That has more to do with historically nourished expectations of prestige, influence, and prosperity—the time-honored luster and appeal of the Harvard brand.

Thus it is no wonder that more than 8,000 candidates compete for admission to the barely 800 places reserved for first-year graduate students, despite the 60,000-dollar price tag that goes with acceptance. Top academic records and top grades on admission tests may be sufficient to get candidates into other schools—Harvard Business School also requires three letters of recommendation.

Yet for most graduates, the degree is more than worth all that money and effort. An MBA degree from Harvard Business School is practically a ticket to the very top in business, public administration, or the political power centers of the world—to those places where what you are depends so much on knowing you belong to the elite.

FAME

*l.a.***E**yeworks®

L.A.
EYEWORKS

BRAND STORY

Gai Gherardi and Barbara McReynolds have lots of admirers: Elton John, Joe Pantoliano, David Hockney, Mick Jagger, Bobby McFerrin, Jeff Goldblum, Udo Kier, Jürgen E. Schrempp, Boy George, Philip Glass, John Waters—to name only a few famous older men. Not to mention the famous young men and the many famous women who also admire the two so much. And why? They all wear eyeglasses by l.a.Eyeworks.

Gai Gherardi and Barbara McReynolds have been making eyeglasses since 1979 and selling them in their own outlets in Los Angeles, but also in faraway lands and cultures as well. The company headquarters in "Dreamworks City," with its Walk of Fame, is the ideal stage for a brand that regards eyeglasses as a form of personal expression and personalities as vehicles of expression for eyeglasses.

The two founders have found a broad theme with an infinite potential for variation. "A face is like a work of art. It deserves a great frame" is the guiding principle and the constant message. They have made it their theme and put their own mark on it. In character studies by photographer Greg Gorman, they shape a public image through which the brand continually renews itself and gains new strength—yet remains ever true to itself. Gai Gherardi and Barbara McReynolds can be proud of themselves and of l.a.Eyeworks.

BRAND PROMISE

ABSOLUTION

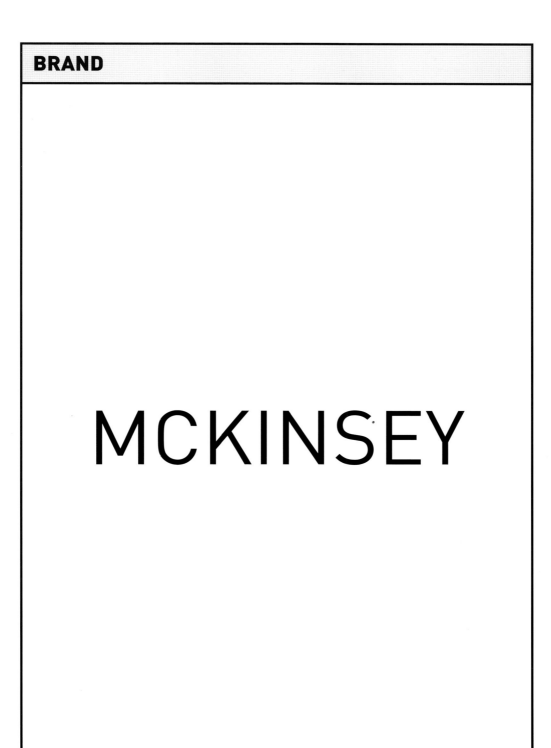

MCKINSEY

BRAND STORY

Lukas Mühlemann was the head of McKinsey & Company in Switzerland. He took on a consulting job for the national airline Swissair and its CEO, Hugo Loepfe. Loepfe followed one of McKinsey's recommendations and bought part interest in Sabena, the foundering Belgian airline. Three and a half years later, Lukas Mühlemann had become CEO of the Credit Suisse Group and a member of the advisory board of Swissair. In his new capacity, he approved the dismissal of Hugo Loepfe, his ex-client, from his job as head of Swissair. Loepfe's successor Philippe Bruggisser commissioned McKinsey & Company again to do a project study. Under the code name "Hunter," McKinsey director Nils Hagander presented a list of strategies designed to help Swissair survive in a deregulated market. Swissair proceeded to acquire interest in several other struggling airlines.

Two and a half years later, Swissair went bankrupt, triggering a national identity crisis in Switzerland and generating negative publicity for McKinsey & Company—unjustly, as many people now feel. After all, people tend to forget when things go wrong that consultants are just consultants and not decision-makers. Consultants sworn to secrecy are usually pulled into the public limelight at times when weak-kneed clients who are incapable of making decisions look to their advisors for absolution and not just for guidance on decisions in matters of business or management policy.

The fact that more firms tend to credit McKinsey & Company with absolutely reliable expertise and good judgment than their competitors is largely attributable to their success. Ever since James Oskar McKinsey began advising top executives of major companies on how to improve their competitive strength in Chicago in 1926, the consulting firm has earned an extraordinary reputation all over the world—in nearly all industries and markets and virtually every field of management. McKinsey & Company have an image that promises top performance and obliges them to deliver on that promise. But it is sometimes linked with expectations that even "Mackies," as McKinsey consultants are nicknamed by some competitors, could meet only if they were convinced of their own infallibility.

McKinsey & Company is an excellent case in point that illustrates how a brand promise can take on a life of its own, one the trademark owner may not be able to influence.

More Books about Brands:

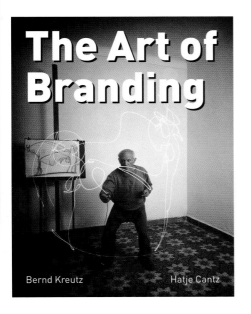

The Art of Branding

Bernd Kreutz   Hatje Cantz

Virtually no other phenomenon has engaged the minds of corporate management
quite like the concept of "brand".
Marketing literature is full of theories and
recommendations on such topics as brand
potential and brand management, brand
value and brand mythology. Yet few pub-
lications address the crucial question of
how brands are made. In marketing as in
art, the art is not in talking about it but in
making it.

"The Art of Branding" traces the career of
Pablo Picasso as an exemplary illustration
of the art of branding.

ISBN 3-7757-9157-4

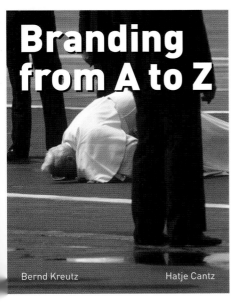

Branding from A to Z

Bernd Kreutz   Hatje Cantz

We live in a world of brands. Brands play
a crucial role in business competition but
have also become an highly significant
phenomenon.

Brands are represented by signs and symbols, gestures and images. They stand for
values, hopes, and desires, for experien-
ces and expectations. They evoke emotions
and associations.

"Branding from A to Z" is a crash course
in the essence and impact of brands from
A to Z.

ISBN 3-7757-9159-0

Concept, text, and design:
Bernd Kreutz

Translation: John Southard
Printed by: Dr. Cantz'sche Druckerei, Ostfildern-Ruit

© 2003 Hatje Cantz Verlag, Ostfildern-Ruit, and Bernd Kreutz

Published by
Hatje Cantz Verlag
Senefelderstraße 12
73760 Ostfildern-Ruit
Germany
Tel. +49 / 7 11 / 4 40 50
Fax +49 / 7 11 / 4 40 52 20
www.hatjecantz.de

Distribution in the US:
D.A.P., Distributed Art Publishers, Inc.
155 Avenue of the Americas, Second Floor
New York, N.Y. 10013-1507
USA
Tel. +1 / 212 / 627 1999
Fax +1 / 212 / 627 9484

ISBN 3-7757-9159-0

Printed in Germany